Help Your Child Succeed in School

A Parent's Primer for Evaluating, Choosing, and Working with Public and Private Schools K-12

Margaret A. Dalia, M.A.

The Clarendon Group, Inc.
Atlanta, Georgia

HELP YOUR CHILD SUCCEED IN SCHOOL

A Parent's Primer for Evaluating, Choosing, and Working with Public and Private Schools K-12

COPYRIGHT © 1989 The Clarendon Group, Inc.

Library of Congress Catalog No: 89-61959

ISBN:1-877816-02-7

Cover design by Terry Tilley

Editing by Andree Harris

First Edition

Printed in the United States of America

Published by The Clarendon Group, Inc., Suite 340, 2480-4 Briarcliff Road, Atlanta, Georgia 30329

Limitations of Liability and Disclaimer of Warranty

To my mother, Sara, my husband, Chris,
and my daughter, Katie

Acknowledgements

My ideas for this book began to take shape more than 20 years ago, when I first became interested in how people learn. Its focus, equipping parents to be effective advocates for helping their children succeed in school, stems from a discussion with my husband, Chris, when we were talking about the problems in our educational system. Chris made several critical points:

> that many of us had lost sight of the purpose of teaching, i.e., helping the students succeed at learning, and,

> that we wouldn't see significant improvements until the consumers (the parents and students) took responsibility for requiring and helping create the improvements.

The recommendations and tools included in this book are a synthesis of effective management and teaching techniques I've acquired through diverse experiences working with adults and children in the United States and other countries.

There are many talented people with whom I have worked and learned, and for whom I feel a great deal of appreciation.

I wish to express special appreciation to the following individuals who assisted in the development of this book.

Chris Dalia, M.A.
Kathie Grubb
Andree Harris
Meredith Hickson, M.P.H.
Franklin Miller
Sara Sloss, M.S.
Nella Stewart
TerryTilley
Patricia Timm, M.B.A.
McWilson Warren, M.S.P.H., Ph.D.

About the Author

Margaret Dalia, M. A., is owner and president of The Clarendon Group, Inc., a management consulting and publishing firm based in Atlanta, Georgia. She has more than 20 years' experience in designing, evaluating and carrying out educational programs. She combines these skills with an extensive background in management and management consulting. Her clients include the U.S. Centers for Disease Control and the World Health Organization, in addition to businesses in the private sector.

*Ms. Dalia has an M.A. degree in Educational Psychology. She is author of **Super Teaching: How to Help Your Students Learn**, a book for individuals who have been asked to teach without having had formal training in education. The book includes step-by-step guidelines for systematically planning and designing effective instructional programs and for enabling the teacher to carry out self-evaluations.*

The author may be reached by writing to:

The Clarendon Group, Inc.
Suite 340
2480-4 Briarcliff Road
Atlanta, Georgia 30329

or by calling 404-284-7012,

or by faxing 404-284-7028.

Contents

Chapter 2: 21

Spell out what you are looking for -- What is right for your child?

Chapter 3: 51

Look around -- Compare what you see with what you are looking for.

Chapter 4: 83

As school is beginning, help your child succeed.

Chapter 5: 101

Report Cards to evaluate schools

Useful References and Resources 119

Ask any questions.

As any educator knows, it is the first step to finding answers.

Introduction

Introduction

Who this book is for

This book is for you, the parent of school-aged children from kindergarten through highschool. You may be moving into a new community or looking at schools for the first time for a young child; or you may be concerned that your child, already in school, may not be doing as well as possible. Or, you just may be interested in making a good school situation even better. Whatever the case, this book should be useful to you in looking at public or private schools.

Why this book was written

This book has been written to help you help your child succeed in school. You are a key person in your child's success. You know your child best. You have the greatest concern for your child succeeding. You are the person ultimately responsible for helping your child succeed and, in fact, your involvement is critical to your child's success.

You and your family members are paying for your child's

education--whether through the taxes you pay or through tuition. You have every right to participate in the decisions about your child's education, and to help ensure that what is done brings out the best in your child.

You may have felt in the past that since you don't have a degree in Education, you don't know as much as the teachers about what is an effective school situation for your child. You may be underestimating your ability to assess your child's situation at school.

The experiences you have in other phases of your life transfer to this situation. At all times, even if you are not sure of yourself, the best thing you can do is to listen to your intuition. While no school situation will be perfect, some may be better suited than others to your child. This book is written to help you clarify your intuitive assessment about what will help your child succeed.

You are not alone in the effort to help your child succeed. There is an ongoing movement of parents getting more involved in the education of their children. In 1985, the State of Minnesota implemented a system in which parents can choose their children's public schools. Rudy Perpich, Governor of Minnesota, in an editorial in the Monday, March 6, 1989, issue of the New York Times, described the rationale for the change and the results. He made the following statements:

> "By embracing choice and open enrollment, we have created an atmosphere in which everyone is taking a closer look at what makes a good school and what accounts for high quality education.

People are making a fresh effort to achieve higher standards.

"The positive spin-offs of choice are many, including more exciting opportunities for teachers, greater support for school levy referendums, better administration of our schools, and higher quality education for our young people.

"But most of all, choice has promoted greater involvement by Minnesota's parents in the education of their children. Ultimately, parents are the ones who must demand quality. They must know what is expected of their children at various levels of education. And they must help set the tone and the attitude of our children toward the value of education.

"By allowing market forces to work in our educational system, families are empowered to make discerning choices about their schools. And they compel schools to be more responsive to the people they serve."

This book is not about the political decisions regarding state laws for giving parents choice. The book is designed to give you the information you need, in ways which will be easy to use, so that you:

are a more informed consumer;

have the criteria you need to ask the right questions, and keep asking;

are able to find out what is expected of your child;

are able to assess whether the teaching is effective;

are able to work constructively with teachers to influence your child's schooling; and

are an effective advocate for your child in order to help your child succeed.

How this book is designed

This book is designed to be easy to use.

Although the book is comprehensive, it is designed so that you can quickly reference the information that will be useful to you at different points of your child's education.

This book includes guidelines for time-saving steps to follow. There are checklists of questions to carry with you when you talk with principals, teachers, and other parents. These can be used as cues for issues you want to address in such situations as when you observe a school, attend school orientations, or participate in parent/ teacher conferences.

There are even report cards for schools, that distill the principles of good teaching and a good school setting contained in the guidelines into easy-to-use worksheets.

This book was written as a result of many conversations with parents who were concerned about their children's education, but unsure of themselves in this arena. They found it difficult to sort through the vocabulary used by educators. This book was designed to clearly express the concepts and technology behind effective instructional design in language understood by non-educators.

Parents assisted in the development of this book by trying it out in different settings to ensure that the tools would be easy to use.

The book is designed to be of immediate use. We have tried to describe concepts in clear terms without educational jargon, yet tried to ensure that the book is substantive enough that you can:

- recognize good teaching when you see it,

- know the right questions to ask,

- proceed in a systematic, time-saving manner, and

- approach problems rationally and constructively.

How to use this book

This book has five chapters.

Chapter One

o   clarifies what the goal is and what should be done to achieve the goal,

o   highlights the purpose of school and important skills to develop at school.

Chapter Two

o   introduces you to the basic building blocks of a good school situation and effective teaching,

o   includes a list of characteristics that may stimulate your thinking about what your child is like.

Chapter Three

o   provides time-saving information on how to identify options in the community in the public and private sectors,

o   describes what information you can request,

o   describes how to evaluate the school and the teaching.

Chapter Four

o   provides guidelines for actions to take to help
        your child succeed once school begins,

o   provides action plans in the event that you have
        concerns about your child's current situation.

Chapter Five

o   addresses your need for easy-to-use Report Cards
        for schools--for summarizing your assessment of
        each school, your assessment of the effectiveness
        of the teaching, and for comparing schools to each
        other.

You may find it helpful to first scan all five chapters.
There is information useful in each chapter regardless of
whether you are trying to make a good school situation
better, solve problems in a difficult school situation,
identify schools in the community, or choose a school.

Then, focus in on the sections that will be most helpful.
Even within individual sections, you may prioritize specific
issues you intend to address at certain points in time.

This book provides you the information you need to be
well-prepared for discussions with principals and teachers.
There are likely to be a variety of responses from the
principals and teachers. Many educators will respect and
appreciate your interest and involvement with your child's
education and will respond rationally to your concerns and
questions.

When individuals respond with respect, you will have a sense of what they would be like to work with during the school year.

If you do find individuals who feel ill at ease with your questions, their feelings may be a result of a number of factors. A teacher may feel you should not be asking the questions or raising the issues. Or the manner in which you are asking the questions may make the teacher feel uneasy.

The issues covered in this book are valid issues; the questions are valid questions. The book has been developed to facilitate your thinking. It is recommended that you use the guidelines and checklists in the same manner--to facilitate the thinking of the teachers, principals, and your child.

Before meeting with a teacher, it may be helpful to ensure that the teacher is sensitive to what you are trying to do (help your child succeed). You may find it helpful to summarize certain sections of this book and share them with the teacher before the next meeting. Let the teacher know that these particular points or issues are important to you and that you would like to discuss them with him/her. You may also want to prepare an informal agenda to share with the teacher prior to your meeting. The agenda should summarize the key issues you want to discuss.

Help Your Child Succeed in School is a blueprint, a plan from which you can work. It is a resource which will be useful at different junctures of your child's educational experience. There is no utopia. You won't be likely to have a school situation that is perfect for your child all of the time. You also won't be likely to have the time to carry out all of the ideas in the book. Do what you can in the time you have. Everything you do is important.

We hope that this book gives you the information you need to help your child succeed in school.

> Margaret A. Dalia
> Atlanta, Georgia

Chapter One

Define your goal and how to achieve it.

Chapter 1

Part 1:
What's the Goal: Helping Your
Child Succeed in School.

What does success mean?

Success means different things to different people.
People have different talents, different ways of learning,
different ways of processing information, different values,
and different interests. Success has to do with your child
reaching his or her fullest potential. Achieving success
begins with building on your child's natural talents and
intrinsic interests. People tend to do best in areas that
they enjoy and in which they have talent.

What is the purpose of school?

Attending school is only one way of learning. To learn is to gain knowledge or understanding of, or skill in something by study, instruction, and/or experience. The purpose of school is to help equip the student to function in an increasingly complicated and rapidly changing society, to perform increasingly complex jobs, to compete in the world economy, and to live with people who represent an increasingly diverse mixture of cultural backgrounds.

What are important skills to learn at school?

Depending on the student's natural talents and interests, the specific skills to be acquired will vary. Listed below are *examples* of skills which equip one to function in our society and which apply in a variety of professions.

Intellectual skills

1. Thinking skills, including analysis, synthesis, evaluation, generalization, and creation.

2. Express ideas in writing clearly, logically, systematically, and persuasively.

3. Express ideas orally clearly, logically, systematically, and persuasively.

4. Express ideas in non-verbal media, e.g., music, art, etc.

5.   Identify practical, efficient means to solve problems and accomplish goals.

6.   Plan, monitor, and make needed adjustments to accomplish goals.

7.   Learn new information, concepts, methodologies, and transfer what is learned to other experiences.

Interpersonal skills

1.   Demonstrate regard for other people's ideas, interests, convenience, and feelings.

2.   Re-evaluate one's position on the basis of new information or rational criticism.

3.   Be dependable.

4.   Persevere at difficult junctures.

Part 2:
What Should You Do to
Achieve Your Goal--to Help
Your Child Succeed?

Keep your eye on the goal.

Keeping this goal in mind is important. It may not always
be easy because you have to work with the "system." An
industrialized society has large systems that emerge to
help organize our efforts. As beneficial as these systems
are, every system is fallible, including school systems. In
addition, the larger the system, the more cumbersome it
becomes for individuals both inside and outside the system
to accomplish something or achieve change. More
policies and operating procedures get established. More
approvals are required to change policies and procedures,
or to do something that hasn't been done before.
Obtaining approvals requires extensive planning and
communication, is very labor-intensive, and takes a long
time to complete. As the parent, your efforts are critical
for helping your child succeed, since others in the sytem
may have conflicting demands and priorities.

Keeping your eye on the goal (helping your child succeed)
will help you work through the school systems, learn about
them, and make the needed changes. You may also find
that coordinating your efforts with teachers and other
parents who share your values and concerns may help
achieve change.

This book is all about what to do to help your child succeed in school. Most importantly, success takes a team effort--on the parts of the student, the teachers and administrators, and the parents. Several things have to be done:

1. *Spell out what you are looking for--in other words-- what is right for your child:*

   in terms of a good school setting,

   in terms of good teaching, and

   in terms of what your child is like and what will bring out the best in your child.

2. *Look around. Compare what you see with what you are looking for.*

   Locate your options. What public and private schools are available? Obtain information about all schools that interest you.

   Evaluate the schools and the effectiveness of the teaching. Use the report cards for schools in Chapter 5 of this book.

3. *As the school year begins--help your child to succeed.*

   You're a critical member of a team effort. Take the lead, plan your strategy, monitor, evaluate, and head off problems.

4. *Address your concerns--promptly and constructively.*

Keep activities and concerns focused on the goal--
to help your child succeed. Focus on the issues
and the future. Identify the problems and possible
solutions. Spell out the goals and specific future
actions. Take the actions you think are necessary
to help your child succeed. You have an
important responsibility to facilitate planning,
monitoring, and problem-solving to help your
child succeed.

Each of these issues is addressed in greater detail
in the following chapters.

Chapter Two

Spell out what you are looking for -- what is right for your child?

Chapter 2

Spell out what you are looking for -- what is right for your child?

The information in Chapter Two is provided to help you define which school setting will bring out the best in your child.

Develop a list of criteria for what is best for your child. Base the list on your child's characteristics. Include in the list a description of the school setting in which you're interested, and key factors in the teaching and in the way the teachers and school relate to your child.

Parts 3, 4, 5, and 6 in this chapter will give you a lot of information from which to work. They include tools designed to stimulate your thinking:

Part 3: What does a good school setting look like?

Part 4: What is teaching?

Part 5: What does good teaching look like?

Part 6: What is your child like and what brings out the best in your child?

Use these tools as working tools and modify them as you see fit to meet your values.

Part 3:
What Does a "Good" School
Setting Look Like?

Before beginning to look for a school, it is important to define what you are looking for. Listed below are a number of factors in a school setting which together increase the likelihood that your child will succeed. These factors are the focal point for all of the guidelines and tools in this book.

1. *Effective teaching techniques are employed.*

2. *Teachers have the time and support of the administration to carry out effective teaching techniques.*

3. *The effort is a team effort--between students, teachers, administrators, and parents. And team members have the same goal: to help the child succeed.*

4. *Team members communicate with each other.*

5. *Team members monitor the progress towards achieving the goal.*

6. *Team members monitor, raise, and address their concerns promptly, forthrightly, and constructively.*

7. *Team members make changes as needed to help achieve the goal: to help the child succeed.*

Part 4:
What is Teaching?

The purpose of teaching

Teaching is a profession, much like engineering, practicing medicine, or painting. Like any profession, it requires specialized knowledge and skills, and often long and intensive preparation. The preparation of a teacher includes instruction in skills and methods as well as principles underlying the skills and methods. *The purpose of teaching is to facilitate learning.* A teacher's responsibility is to provide an environment in which students can acquire needed skills and knowledge.

Instruction should be planned

Planning a well-designed course or curriculum (a whole body of courses offered by an educational institution) begins with defining in very clear terms what are called "instructional objectives." These objectives are, in essence, the destination on a roadmap, and include very specific descriptions of the following:

a.   The performance or behavior that will be
        expected of the student at the end of the course.

b.   Under what conditions the student will be
        performing (e.g., with access to the following
        references . . .).

c.   The criteria that will be used to evaluate the
        student's performance.

Instructional objectives can be written for any subject
matter, whether it is tangible subject matter (such as
carrying out basic mathematics) or abstract subject matter
(such as analyzing English literature).

Trying to perform well in a class without instructional
objectives is like trying to drive a car across a country you
are visiting for the first time without being told your
destination, much less when you should arrive, what laws
and customs you should follow, and useful hints and
shortcuts: you wouldn't know where you were headed or
what to do and the likelihood is low that you arrive where
you should on time and according to the laws.

A well-designed course or curriculum includes a clear and
logical arrangement of multiple activities. These
activities, in turn, should result in learning what is spelled
out in the instructional objectives.

The activities include:

> provision of information, concepts, and guidelines orally or in writing,
>
> demonstration of examples,
>
> practice (opportunities to apply the concepts), and
>
> exchanges with others about what is and is not understood.

The selection of activities varies, depending on the age and competencies of the students, and the skills, knowledge, and understanding to be acquired. However, a well-designed course or curriculum uses a combination of teaching methods in order to help learning occur.

In a well-designed course, the majority of students can succeed.

A few key teaching methods

There are many different specific techniques that can be used to teach. These techniques can be categorized within six basic methods for teaching. All of these methods, if used correctly and together, can facilitate learning.

These teaching methods, their primary purposes, and their advantages and disadvantages are listed below:

1. **Provide information orally, such as through a lecture.**

    Purpose:

    Provide information, concepts, guidelines, and examples.

    Advantages:

    Lectures provide an opportunity for teachers to give an overview, an orientation.

    Lectures also provide an opportunity for teachers to convey enthusiasm and appreciation for a subject.

    Disadvantages:

    Students may stop listening after a short period of time because they are not actively participating. Younger children won't listen for an extended period of time. Even many adult learners listen for only brief periods of time.

    Lecturing can be an inefficient method of communicating information. Individuals can often read the same information in a fraction of the time.

During a lecture, students cannot move at their own pace. Those who already understand the subject find the pace too slow. (You can't fast-forward a lecturer!) They lose interest. Those who lack a great deal of critical background information may get behind in their assimilation of the new information and concepts. They get behind and then get lost. They, too, lose interest.

Students can leave a lecture thinking they understand. However, understanding words is very different from understanding what happens when the ideas are applied. Without an opportunity to apply the concepts, students do not discover what they do and do not understand.

2. **Provide opportunities to acquire information by reading.**

Purpose:

Provide information, concepts, guidelines, and examples.

Advantages:

Acquiring information by reading can take less time than listening to a lecture and taking notes.

Reading enables students to move at their own pace.

Disadvantages:

Students can read about concepts and think they understand. Without an opportunity to apply the concepts, they may not discover what they do and do not understand.

3.   **Demonstration**

Purpose:

Show how to apply information and concepts. Demonstration can provide a model for both how to correctly carry out activities and for what incorrect performance looks like.

Advantages:

Demonstration can be used effectively to convert words to reality.

Demonstration increases what students understand.

Disadvantages:

Demonstration does not provide the same understanding and skills that the opportunity to practice through application does.

4. Practice -- Opportunities to apply concepts to encourage thinking

Purpose:

Provides students with opportunities to apply information and concepts in practice sessions.

Application entails the students actually carrying out the activities themselves. As they apply information, rules, and guidelines that they hear, read, and/or see, students have to think about what they are doing:

> They have to **evaluate**: to compare a set of circumstances to a set of criteria.

> They have to **synthesize**: to pull together into a coherent form elements which were not clearly tied together.

> They have to **analyze**: to break something complicated into its parts.

> They have to **create**: to make something that was not there before.

In order to make all of the decisions required in thinking, one is forced to come to grips with what seems clear, but is not.

Application can take many forms--whether it is written, oral, musical, etc. It can be done

 individually or with others,

 in a role-play situation, in which the complexity of the situation can be controlled, and

 in an on-the-job situation, which usually is less controllable and more complicated.

Regardless of the form, the purpose is to have an opportunity to take what one has heard, read about, or seen, and make use of it to see such things as whether it is suitable, or whether and how it fits.

Advantages:

Students become actively involved, which increases interest.

Application requires thinking (e.g., comparison of situations to rules or principles, breaking something up into its elements, pulling elements together, or creating something not there before).

Disadvantages:

May be harder to implement when the teacher has
too many students. Application takes more time
than disseminating information. Application
requires more effort on the part of the teacher.

5. Communication between students and teachers, and between students and students

Purpose:

Communication entails sharing thoughts and
understanding each other's ideas. Communication
is a two-way street between people. It consists of
listening, as well as talking, by all parties.
Effective communication should result in changes
in actions by both parties. The ultimate purpose
of the communication is to help the student
succeed. Communication in this setting consists of
actions such as the following:

> listening by the student to understand
> what the teacher is saying;
>
> questioning from the student that tries to
> get at what is not understood;
>
> listening by the teacher to understand
> what the student is saying;
>
> discussion of issues the student has not

understood to increase understanding;

discussion of changes that could be made in what the student is doing and/or what the teacher is doing;

feedback from the teacher on the student's performance according to the instructional objectives;

thinking by the teacher about factors which could have possibly contributed to the lack of understanding. Examples of these include, but are not limited to:

>the clarity of what performance or behavior is expected of the student;
>
>the clarity of the original presentation of the information, concepts, and guidelines;
>
>the effectiveness of the examples and demonstrations;
>
>whether there have been sufficient opportunities to practice and sufficient feedback.

Advantages:

Communication has a very powerful impact on what students understand and their skill development. It is critical to learning actually taking place.

Also, communication gives needed information to help ensure that students and teachers make changes so that future students can learn more effectively.

Disadvantages

Communication is harder to carry out when a teacher has too many students. It takes more time and effort on the part of the teachers and students.

Communication also requires the teacher and the students to be open-minded and objective about the situation.

If communication is not specific and constructive (e.g., merely a grade on a test with wrong answers circled), students will not know what they need to do differently. All they know is that they will need to answer the question differently. Also, changes will not be made in the instruction to help create a more effective instructional setting for future students.

6. Testing

Purpose:

Testing is not actually a requirement for learning, although it does have several useful purposes.

Testing enables teachers to monitor the progress of students and to document in an explicit manner the extent to which students have learned.

This information is useful to diagnose difficulties and to determine not only what the students should do differently, but also how the teacher should modify the design of the instruction or the teaching.

Advantages:

Testing provides a system of accountability.

It provides a system for identifying and diagnosing problems in the methods used for learning and teaching.

Testing also enables teachers to see patterns in how students are learning both as individuals and as a group. Seeing the patterns helps the teacher determine needed changes in the design of the instruction or in the teaching.

Disadvantages:

Tests scores may become the focal point in school, instead of learning.

Testing can be misused in a number of ways:

> The criteria to be used to evaluate the student's performance may not be made explicit prior to the test.
>
> The activities during the test and/or the criteria used to evaluate these activities may differ from previous practice exercises.
>
> Tests may be used without opportunities to practice the skills being evaluated.
>
> Poor performance may be interpreted as a failure on the student's part instead of as a stimulus for problem solving (such as remediation or modifying the instruction).
>
> The grades on tests may be based on how students did in relation to each other, rather than on how well they performed the skills according to specified criteria. Thus, the focus on helping ensure that the student acquires certain skills, knowledge, and understanding is lost, since grades do not reflect skill acquisition and learning.

Part 5:
What Does Good
Teaching Look Like?

As mentioned in Part 4, a variety of teaching techniques
can be used, depending on such factors as

> the age, skills, and knowledge of the students,

> what is to be taught,

> and the way individual students learn.

Regardless of the age and backgrounds of the students,
there are some basic principles of "good" teaching. There
are certain factors within the teacher's control that
contribute to students successfully learning. These
factors are criteria you can use to assess the schools.
Again, it is important to keep in mind the goal: to help
the student succeed. Good teaching facilitates learning.

Good teaching takes into account how people learn.

Even though people have some things in common, we
take in the world around us differently.

Each of us perceives, processes, and remembers life's stimuli in our own ways.

In addition, people enter learning situations with different degrees of understanding of different aspects of the subject matter.

Often, people don't learn new information and concepts in a perfectly logical sequence. During the process of learning, people acquire new information; think about it; create a skeleton of things understood; acquire new information; try to attach it to the skeleton, modify the skeleton; etc.; etc.

Also, people can only take in a certain amount of new information at one time. The extent to which such assimilation happens depends on each of us as individuals and our prior exposure to similar areas.

When entering new territory, people need more cues. As the concepts are grasped, fewer cues are needed.

The learning process is a combination of new and familiar experiences. People explore new territory, and reach their limits as to what they can take in at that moment. They return to familiar territory and practice what is known to increase proficiency, then venture out again into new territory.

Good teaching is focused -- for everyone concerned.

Good teaching defines in very clear terms:

what will be expected of the student at the
end of the course,

under what conditions, and

what criteria will be used to evaluate the student's
performance.

Together, the performance expected, the conditions one
is to work under, and the criteria form an "instructional
objective."

Good teaching informs students at the beginning of the course what performance is expected of them.

The instructional objectives (the performance expected,
the conditions one is to work under, and the criteria to be
used for evaluating performance) are explicitly stated and
given to students at the beginning of a course.

The instructional objectives should be written in terms
that are clear to the new learner. If students are too
young to understand the objectives, then the objectives
should be accessible in writing and perfectly clear to you,
the parent.

Good teaching uses students' time effectively, rather than
creating a game in which the students are spending time
trying to figure out what the teacher wants.

Good teaching creates an environment in which the majority of students can succeed.

Courses are designed with an understanding of the skills and knowledge with which the majority of students enter the course. Thus, the objectives, practice, feedback, and tests ensure that the *majority* of students can succeed (can acquire the skills and knowledge). In addition, the skills and knowledge to be acquired should be beyond the current understanding of the majority of the students.

For the learning experience to be successful, a course must be designed so that, for the individual:

> It is satisfying (there is sufficient complexity, e.g., new information or concepts, to be challenging). If this does not happen, the person gets bored.

> **and**

> It is enjoyable. There is not so much complexity (e.g., new information or concepts) that the student does not have the time to organize, sort out, ask questions, and develop an understanding before moving on. If this happens, the person gets overloaded, lost, and then frustrated and/or bored.

Good teaching is realistic.

The instructional objectives (the skills and knowledge to be acquired) are based on the amount of time the majority of students have to dedicate to the course. This linkage ensures that the instructional objectives are feasible.

Good teaching ensures active participation. It fosters application of concepts in order to develop thinking, understanding, and skills.

Application of concepts and knowledge enhances the learning process.

There is a difference between passive and active learning. Passive learning entails seeing, listening to, or reading about an issue or process. Active learning goes beyond that initial step. Following the initial exposure, the student has an opportunity to apply the information or concepts.

Retention comes from usage. If students merely memorize and repeat back specific facts, their retention (and their learning) is minimal. If, on the other hand, students are given a body of knowledge and are required to develop a sufficient understanding of the knowledge to apply it, e.g., to make a decision or an assessment, they gradually learn it.

Good teaching increases proficiency by varying experiences.

The more situations in which the student has to apply the rules and principles, the more skill the student develops. Expertise results from the individuals applying the rules in a sufficient number of varied situations, that they begin to understand when to apply the rules and principles, and when to modify them to work in real situations.

Good teaching tries to meet the needs of individual students.

Students differ in their entry skills, their skills at learning, and the pace at which they think and work. Good teaching allows for these differences and facilitates learning for each person. For those who do not fit neatly into the "majority" of students for whom the course is designed, remedial *or* supplemental action is taken, as needed, to address individual needs.

Good teaching provides prompt, effective, and constructive feedback.

Feedback is a response from the teacher following a review of the work. Effective feedback is prompt, specific, and constructive. The feedback provides specific suggestions for improvements and specific comments on aspects done well. A grade alone will not give the student the information needed to know what changes to make.

Good teaching encourages students to communicate promptly what they do not understand -- and then helps the student understand.

Discussions between the student and teacher should include opportunities for 1) the students to ask questions about what they still do not understand and 2) the teachers to answer these questions in a non-judgmental and clear manner. Such discussions are essential for learning to occur.

Good teaching has continuity between what is supposed to be learned, what is taught, and what is tested.

The information provided, the guidelines given, the opportunities to practice, the feedback, and the tests should all be related to the instructional objectives. In fact, the tests should match the instructional objectives. An assessment of the students' success should not be based on surprises. Students' performance should be evaluated according to what they were told would be expected of them, not new information, concepts, or actions.

Good teaching uses tests to monitor student progress in order to help students succeed.

Tests provide valuable information to the teacher, and not just information on how a particular student is doing. If a student does not perform well, it is not necessarily a failure of the student. Good teaching uses tests as diagnostic tools--both of students and the instruction. The teacher may want to re-examine and modify the course design and/or the instructional methods. Or the teacher can use the results of tests as indicators about where remedial or supplemental teaching may be needed. Tests should be a means to prevent students from failing.

Good teaching ensures that grades reflect what is and isn't learned, rather than how students are doing in relation to each other.

Good teaching allows the students to demonstrate the degree to which they have acquired knowledge, understanding, or skills.

Grades may be an inevitability of large and complex societies. However, grades should reflect how each individual student performs in relation to the defined instructional objectives, rather than how students perform in relation to each other.

If *all* students can demonstrate that they have acquired the skills, knowledge, and understanding according to the criteria in the instructional objectives, they should *all* succeed and they should all have "good grades."

Students' successes and failures should be a result of their performance in relation to the instructional objectives, not a result of how their test scores are statistically related to the test scores of their co-students.

Part 6:
What is Your Child Like? What Will Bring out the Best in Him or Her?

This section is not designed to enable you to do a psychological study of your child. It is designed to trigger some thoughts to help you think about your child. You know your child. This section will enable you to have the words, as you need them, to effectively represent your child with principals and teachers.

Each of us is different. Following is a checklist that includes some of the ways in which we differ. Think about your child in relation to these and any other factors that seem important to you.

Student's interests/likes and dislikes

Student tends to focus in on one area *or* student's interests are diverse. Specific examples of interests include music, painting, mathematics, reading, athletics, computers, competitive sports, individual sports, etc.

What student values

Student's standards for his/her own performance

exceed most others *or* student's standards are
similar to others.

Student finds particular consequences rewarding,
for example:

> to some, good grades are important; to
> some, they are not;

> to some, a teacher's opinions are
> important; to some, to a lesser degree;

> to some, fitting into a group of peers is
> important; to some, to a lesser degree.

How student relates to adults

Student asks questions, listens to the answers,
applies the information as needed and makes
decisions for him-or herself *or* student accepts
facts and theories presented without question.

How student relates to other students

Student gets feelings hurt or gets offended easily
or student readily brushes off others' comments.

How student learns

Student learns best by learning rules while
"playing"/experimenting *or* student learns best by
observing, being taught rules, and then "playing."

Student likes figuring things out from scratch *or* student likes a more structured situation in which a great deal of orientation is provided.

Student's degree of self-direction

Student has a great deal of self-direction in terms of things he/she wants to do *or* student more often gets direction from others.

Student's type and degree of intellectual and interpersonal skills

Student is entering school with intellectual or interpersonal skills different from the majority and will require special attention in those areas.

Student is particularly gifted in specific areas, such as music, art, drama, mathematics, computer, athletics, etc.

Chapter Three

Look around--
compare what you see with
what you are looking for

Chapter 3

Part 7:
Locate the Options:
Public and Private Schools

There are a variety of educational alternatives in the community--in both public and private schools, and there is a great deal of information available on both.

Tips for Identifying Private Schools

Private schools are likely to be listed in the yellow pages of the telephone directory under "Schools." In addition, talk with co-workers, friends, and neighbors to identify private schools.

Timing is important in looking for private schools, since there is a specific period each year during which many schools accept applications and get to know prospective students and their parents. Find out, for your community:

a.   when private schools encourage applications,

b.   when the final applications are due, and

c.   when and how admissions tests are given, and how much they cost.

Tips for Identifying Public Schools

In some cities, if your child attends public school, he or she must do so in the community in which you are a taxpayer. In other communities, you can place your child in other school systems by paying a nominal tuition. Find out what is possible in your community by talking with other parents and by contacting the school systems.

You can request information about public schools from the boards of education of various school districts. Each school district decides what and how much information will be provided to the public. On the following pages is a checklist that specifies the information that may be available from a school district or local school system.

The information included in the checklist is in the public domain, meaning that it is accessible to the public. This fact is relevant when you are trying to assess a school district and the information provided is fairly general. For example, the packet of information provided by a school district may include only the average overall test scores for the district. You will need more specific information in order to evaluate individual schools. Information on scores for each school is in the public domain, and therefore should be provided to you upon request.

Information You Can
Request on Public Schools

You can obtain information from individual school districts or city school systems. You can also obtain information at an overview level from the State (or in Canada, the Provincial) department of education. Listed below is a synthesis of information provided by various school systems. You can decide which information will be most helpful to you.

Description of school district

- Map of school district

- Demographic information

Description of schools

- Map of school district with school locations identified

- Directory of all schools in the district

- Per pupil expenditure by the district

- Enrollment information, including demographic information

- Information on personnel, including data on advanced degrees and salaries of faculty

- Policies and procedures, including attendance, transportation, disciplinary policies, severe weather guide, school lunch information, transfer policies, etc.

- Student/teacher ratios at all grades (Check on the number of students and teachers in specific classrooms.)

- Description of recent and approved upcoming facility renovations and expansions for the next several years

- Description of recent and approved upcoming programmatic expansions and changes

- Fiscal information, e.g., annual report, which describes the financial health of the school or school system

- Statistics reflecting student attendance

- Statistics reflecting turnover of students and teachers each year

Student and post-graduate accomplishments

- Requirements for graduation

- Test scores by <u>school</u> as well as by school district

- Test scores by <u>school district</u> (You will have to request specifically by <u>school.</u>) Are the test scores analyzed in a useful way so that you understand the implications of the scores?

- Summary of post-graduate activities (e.g., percentage of students who attend college)

Description of admission procedures and requirements

- Admission requirements

- Health requirements, such as immunizations

- Description of statewide assessment program, e.g., tests required

Description of educational programs and activities

- Description of overall educational program in the school district

- School calendar

- Description of after-school programs for various ages

- Description of elementary school and secondary school programs (Do the descriptions include specific information on subject areas as well as the philosophy of education?)

- Description of special programs in the school district, such as:

  special resources available to students
  special magnet programs
  special programs for international students
  programs for special-needs students
  computer-aided learning programs
  occupational education programs
  technical education programs

guide to advanced placement programs
adopt-a-school programs
programs for "at-risk" students
adult education programs
bi-lingual programs

- Description of any awards received

How to gather more information

- A list of names of individuals to whom you should communicate your ideas and concerns. The list contains the names and phone numbers of individuals such as the principals and the members of the Board of Education.

Parental involvement

- Description of activities to encourage parent involvement

- Description of activities to communicate with parents

- Sample newsletters

Part 8:
Evaluate the schools

Regardless of your circumstances, whether you are trying to make a good situation better, address your concerns at the current school, or seek alternatives, the information in this part will be useful to you. Part 8 has three sections:

Time-saving tips

Questions to ask to evaluate a school

Questions to ask to evaluate the effectiveness of the teaching

Time-saving Tips

When evaluating which school might be best for your child, it is helpful to use a variety of techniques. Whichever techniques you choose to use, it is critical that you feel free to ask questions.

People who work in any specialty area develop a language that has meaning to others in that area. After a while, it is forgotten that the special words are not understandable to people outside of the specialty. This occurs in the profession of Education as well as in other professions.

You may not have had formal training or experience in the field of Education, in which case you may not understand some of the jargon used. You should feel free to ask questions about anything you don't understand or in which you are interested. If you don't understand the answer to your question, ask again. Communication between you and the teacher or principal can occur only if you clarify what you don't understand.

You should end discussions feeling comfortable with your understanding of what has been said and with the resolution of any concerns. Keep the goal in mind (helping your child succeed) in order to keep discussions on track.

1.   *Narrow the search for schools by gathering some of the information over the phone.*

Call ahead to ask questions that may help you eliminate some schools and save you time. Try to get a "bird's-eye" view of the school by talking with key officials, such as the principal.

2.   *Divide the work with some of your friends.*

Come to agreement on the information you are interested in and divide up calls among your friends to schools of mutual interest.

3.   *Schedule appointments to talk and meet with school officials when <u>they</u> have time to meet with you.*

Certain periods of the year are extremely busy. Try to avoid gathering your in-depth information during these busy times. Busy periods include holidays and open-house orientation sessions. (In many communities, the open-house orientations are in January and February.)

Also, find out when the private schools are conducting their preliminary interviews with parents and students. These periods are also very busy and staff may not be able to spend as much time with you as you would like, since they have so many parents to meet.

4.   *Talk with the principal and the appropriate teachers.*

In addition to gathering the information you want, assess how the principal and teachers make you feel as you are learning about the school. These interactions may give you important cues as to how you and your child may be treated.

Some cues to look for and listen to include the following:

      a.   Do you understand their answers?

      b.   If you don't understand, do they make you feel comfortable when you ask them what they mean?

      c.   When you ask for clarification, do they paraphrase their answers in words that you do understand?

      d.   Do they listen to and address the issues you raise, such as your child's characteristics and style of learning?

e.   Do you feel that there is an exchange
        between you and the other person that
        results in both of you understanding the
        other more clearly?

5.   *If you are still interested in a particular school, set up*
        appointments for visiting and observing the school
        and the class.

Choose a time that will give you a view that is fairly
representative. For example, avoid a field-trip day or the
day before Thanksgiving, when fewer children than
normal will be there. An appointment ahead of time
should ensure that the principal and the appropriate
teachers have time to meet with you.

6.   *Observe the appropriate classes in action. Walk*
        around the school and observe the teachers and
        children in action.

As long as you make appointments and avoid intruding on
the classes, the school representatives should make you
feel welcome to spend a long enough time to obtain a
good sense of the class and the teacher(s).

Spend a long enough time that:

        the students and teacher begin to forget about
        your being there, and;

        you see the teacher in varied and difficult
        situations, such as when assisting a student who

learns at a different pace than the rest of the class or when disciplining a student who has acted inappropriately.

Create an observation experience that meets your needs. The time may be as short as an hour or you may spend much of a morning or afternoon. You may decide to return for an additional visit a different day. Or you may decide to also observe classes with children older than yours to assess the degree of skills acquired.

Sit and watch and jot down what you are seeing. Your observation may give you information that enables you to immediately arrive at a conclusion; however, there is no need to feel pressure. You should feel free to reserve judgement. Give yourself time, e.g., overnight, to think about what you saw in relation to your child's needs before arriving at a conclusion. Also, seeing different schools may influence your opinion about any one school. You will learn from each experience.

7.   *Talk with parents and with their children who are enrolled in a particular school or class.*

It may be helpful to ask to speak with parents who have children similar to yours.

8.   *Participate in any formally-scheduled interviews.*

When you are exploring private schools you will find that the schools in a community organize interview sessions. You are likely to first meet with the principal and/or a teacher without your children. A follow-up meeting with your child will probably then be scheduled.

Questions to Ask to Evaluate a School

Following is a list of questions that parents might ask when evaluating whether a school is right for their child. You can ask these questions of principals, teachers, and other parents. Chapter 5 includes several report cards you can use to summarize the information and your assessment of the schools. Use Report Card 2 to summarize information about each school. In addition, Report Card 3 can be used to compare schools to each other.

Student and Post-Graduate Accomplishments

1. What are the tests used to assess the students' achievement? What are the test results for the previous five years? How do these test results compare to those for other schools in the local area? In the state? In the nation?

2. If a secondary school, how many students have left prior to graduation during the last three years? For what reasons?

3. If a secondary school, what does the data show regarding what graduates do, e.g., what percentage attend college? Which colleges do they attend?

Teacher Performance

4. What criteria does the school set for good teaching?

5. Are these criteria distributed in writing to each of the teachers so that they know the standards?

6. What actions does the school take to cultivate good teaching?

   a. What methods does the principal use to monitor and evaluate the teachers' performance to determine whether they are meeting the standards and what improvements could be made?

   b. How frequently is each teacher's performance evaluated in an academic year?

   c. What actions does the principal take following the evaluation:

      Does the principal meet with the teacher and tell the teacher what is being done well and what needs to be improved?

      Does the principal follow up that meeting with additional monitoring and discussions to provide needed guidance and ensure effective teaching?

How many times during the academic year does the principal meet with each teacher to discuss performance?

d.   How does the principal identify problems and what does the principal do to track the problems and ensure that they are solved?

e.   In addition, what actions does the principal take to encourage and support good teaching?

Parental Involvement

7.   Request a copy of any guide the school has for parental involvement. What percentage of the parents are members of any parent organization? Request the names of any organized parent or parent/teacher groups. What activities does the group sponsor? Request the name and phone number of the chairperson of any parents' group. Request the names and phone numbers of parents of children in specific classrooms. Call active parents with an organized set of questions you want to ask them.

8.   What actions does the teacher want the parents to take to encourage learning at home?

9. What type of involvement do the teacher and administration want from the parents?

10. What actions does the teacher take to communicate with the parents and to learn about their concerns? Ask for a copy of any newsletters.

11. Ask whom you should contact when you have concerns, questions, etc. Find out what procedures should be used in the event that you feel that you and the teacher are not communicating effectively.

12. How do the principal/teachers make you feel as you are learning about the school?

Discipline

13. What is the school policy in relation to maintaining discipline?

14. What actions does the teacher take to maintain discipline? If a child is experiencing problems, which staff members other than the teacher and principal are available for consultation?

School Resources

15.   What is the student/teacher ratio for your child's classroom? (Ensure the ratio reflects the actual number of teachers in the classroom, not additional staff, such as the librarian, etc.)

16.   What is the anticipated increase or decrease in the student population during the next five years? What actions is the school planning to take to address any anticipated change?

17.   What plans are there for facility renovations and expansion? What plans are there for programmatic expansion? How much in the way of financial assessments have been made to parents during the last five years? What financial assessments are anticipated during the next five years? What fund-raising activities have occurred in the last five years? What fund-raising activities are planned?

18.   If a private school, is this a permanent facility or leased space? If leased, does the school have plans for a permanent facility? If so, what plans does the school have for raising money for a permanent facility?

19.   Is there a library? How well is it equipped?

20.   Request data reflecting the demographics of the student population, the attendance, and the teacher and student turnover rates.

Educational Opportunities

21.   What language, music, or fine arts programs exist? To what extent are they available? How effective are they: do the children develop the skills?

22.   What physical education/athletic programs are conducted? What athletic facilities exist?

23.   How is the school developing the students' computer skills? What is the student/computer ratio? How many hours per day can a student use the computer? In what ways are computers being used? How effective at skill development are the software programs being used?

24.   What do the principal and teachers consider to be the strengths of the school program? What areas need improvement? What specific actions are being taken to solve any problems and what is the timetable for those actions?

25.   What textbooks are used? What criteria were used to select them? What actions does the teacher take to supplement the activities in the textbooks?

26.   What special programs exist, e.g., for special-needs children? Are bi-lingual or immersion programs available?

27.   Is after-school care available? What are the hours? What experiences are provided during the

after-school program? How much does it cost?

28.   Is there a summer school program? What are the hours? What are the programmatic activities? How much does it cost?

Transportation Arrangements

29.   What arrangements does the school provide to facilitate transportation of students to and from school?

Application/Admission

30.   If a private school, what are the criteria for acceptance into the school?

31.   If a public school, are students accepted from other school districts?

32.   At what grade must the student enter in order to be admitted?

33.   What steps (e.g., completing an application form, sending in fee, participating in parent/child interviews, taking tests, etc.) must the parent and student carry out in order to apply? What deadlines exist for any of the steps?

34.   Are there any costs associated with the

application? If so, what are the costs? When is
payment due? Are there alternative financial
arrangements? Is tuition refundable? If so, under
what conditions?

35.　What tests are required? How and when are they
administered? Is the parent present (for the
younger child)? How much do they cost? Are you
given copies of the results of the tests? If not, why
not?

Costs

36.　Expenses:

Application fee:	_____
Application testing fee:	_____
Annual tuition:	_____
Registration fee:	_____
Books and supplies:	_____
Uniforms, if required:	_____
Transportation arrangements:	_____
After-school care:	_____
Summer school:	_____
Administration fees:	_____
e.g., for paying tuition over time	
Other fees: e.g., art, field trips, etc.	_____
Total	_____

37.   When must tuition be paid? What are the
        methods for payment?

38.   Are financial scholarships available? What are the
        application procedures and deadlines? If you are
        looking at a private school in Canada, through
        what grades are there government subsidies?

Parochial Schools

39.   Is the school affiliated with a particular religious
        denomination? What is it? What religious
        training is provided? How is the training
        provided?

40.   Are students of other religions admitted? What
        arrangements are made for students not of the
        same religion, e.g., during religious education
        classes?

Questions to Ask to Evaluate
the Effectiveness of the Teaching

This section includes questions you can use during parent/
teacher conferences and observations that will enable you
to assess the effectiveness of the teaching. The list of
questions addresses factors that contribute to an effective
instructional program.

The manner in which you ask the questions will affect
your success. You will be more successful if your manner
indicates your interest in contributing to your child's
success rather than in trying to interrogate the teacher.

You may not need to ask all of these questions. You may
not feel comfortable asking all of them. You may not
have time to ask all of them. The questions are organized
to be cues from which you can work. Often some of these
issues will be raised by the teachers and the principals,
and you won't have to ask the questions directly.

Design of the Instruction and Instructional Materials

1.   Have instructional objectives been developed?

        Instructional objectives are specific descriptions of
        performance expected (the skills and knowledge
        with which the majority of students should leave
        the class) and the conditions under which the

students will have to perform. Instructional objectives also include a description of the criteria that will be used to evaluate the performance.

Ask to see the instructional objectives. There should be objectives available for academic, physical education, and social skills. If they are not available in writing, draw the teacher out as to what performance is expected of the students and what the criteria are for evaluating that performance.

Begin anywhere when trying to understand the instructional objectives. Use any words you are comfortable with. Ask what the purpose of the course is. What are the reasons for the different activities? What does the teacher expect of the students? What skills does the teacher expect the students to acquire? What is the outcome of the teaching?

Ask enough questions to feel you understand what is expected of the students, under what conditions, and according to what criteria.

2. Have the skills and knowledge with which the **majority** of students are entering the course been identified? Is the course design based on an understanding of these skills and knowledge?

Ask for a description of the skills and knowledge
with which the majority of students enter the class.
If a description is not available in writing, again
draw the teacher out in order for you to develop
an understanding.

Ideally, teachers have sufficient time to work with
each student. However, in many schools, teachers
have so many students they do not find it possible
to individualize the instruction for all of the
different students.

In these settings, the instructor generally begins
by targeting his/her teaching to a specific range of
entry knowledge and skills and moves at one pace.
The focus is essentially determined by the entry
skills and knowledge of the majority of the
students in the class.

Determine what general range of skills and
knowledge the majority of the students have, and
assess how your child fits in relation to that range.

If you are considering enrolling (or have enrolled)
your child in a setting in which the teachers have
so many children that they lack the time to
provide a significant degree of individual attention
(which may be the majority of schools), try to
choose a school in which the entry level of
knowledge and skills and the instructional pace
approximate those of your child.

3. Are the instructional objectives available and provided in writing (or related orally, if the students are too young to read) to the students at the beginning of the course so that they know what is expected of them?

    Ask to see the materials distributed to the students at the beginning of the course.

4. Are the instructional objectives written in terms that require students to think (to apply information and concepts rather than to merely recite back information)?

    Review the instructional objectives to make this assessment.

    Ask friends whose children are in the school if you can review their children's practice exercises and tests to see if thinking is being cultivated.

Day-to-Day Instructional Experiences

5. Is the instruction related to the instructional objectives? In other words, are all of the following related to the instructional objectives: the information provided, the guidelines, the demonstrations, and the practice exercises?

Review lecture notes, practice exercises, and the feedback provided to the students to assess whether there is continuity between those and the objectives.

6.   Are there sufficient opportunities to practice applying what is being taught so that the students can acquire the skills according to the criteria in the instructional objectives?

Assess whether class activities provide students the opportunities to apply the principles, rules, guidelines, etc., so that they acquire actual skills.

7.   How proficient do the students become?

Speed comes with proficiency. Proficiency comes with practice and feedback. Review the materials and observe the classes to assess the number and variety of opportunities the student has to develop proficiency.

8.   Are students given a sufficient number of opportunities to practice and provided feedback in between practice exercises so that they have the opportunity to improve?

Listen to the interactions between students and teachers, and review the assignments, practice exercises, and tests.

9.   Are students given feedback that is specific and constructive?

Listen to interactions between the students and teachers, and review the exercises and tests to assess whether the feedback includes specific descriptions of aspects well done and specific suggestions for improvements.

10. Are students encouraged to ask questions about what they still do not understand? Do answers appear to be clear? Does the manner in which the answers are given appear non-judgmental?

Listen to the interactions between students and their teachers and co-students. Assess whether the students are encouraged to ask questions about what they still do not understand. Do answers appear to be clear and non-judgmental?

Assessment of Student Progress

11. To what extent does the assessment of student progress relate to the instructional objectives for the academic year? Do the tests match the instructional objectives?

Compare the tests to the instructional objectives. The tests should match the instructional objectives. The tests should not include anything that the teacher did not indicate was to be learned. The grade should not be based on activities or criteria that were not provided at the beginning of the course.

12. Are grades based on how well students performed, and, thus, reflect their achievements?

   Ask the teacher to describe how grades are determined. Determine what the grades are based on. Are they based on how students perform in relation to the defined objectives? Or is there a scale by which the teacher perceives that statistically only a limited number of students can get A's *and* by which a certain number of students *must* fail. Remember the goal is to help the student succeed. Such a statistical scale is not supportive of that goal.

13. Do the teachers hold students responsible for performing?

Extent to Which Individual Student Needs are Met

14. Do the teachers give feedback on individual work often? Does the feedback seem at the appropriate level for each student?

15. Do the teachers keep up with each individual's progress? Do the teachers adjust the techniques for each individual, as appropriate?

   At any point that the student is exceeding or not keeping up with the expected checkpoints of progress, what actions do the teachers take to help ensure the child succeeds? Ask for specific examples of instances and descriptions of actions taken and results.

Again, in many circumstances, the teachers may have so many students that it is not feasible for them to provide one-on-one tutoring. However, the teacher should be monitoring students' progress closely enough to know when a student is getting behind in skill acquisition, or is exceeding the instructional objectives. When such a situation is identified, you and the teacher together can figure out a strategy to help the child succeed.

16. Do the teachers appear to **not** be rigidly bound to one method of teaching? Do they adjust teaching techniques based on what is (and what is **not**) working with a particular student?

Extent to Which Thinking is Encouraged

17. Do the teachers seem to be encouraging thinking? Do they first provide information, then give examples and demonstrations, and then give opportunities to practice applying what the students have heard, read, or seen?

18. Do the teachers help students learn where to look for information and answers to their questions, rather than emphasizing memorization of facts independent of thinking?

Manner of the Teacher

To what extent does the teacher:

19.   act friendly and non-threatening?

20.   encourage students to ask questions?

21.   listen to questions students ask and provide
       relevant answers?

22.   respond in a non-judgmental manner with ideas
       appropriate for the students' level, rather than
       talking down to the students?

23.   appear interested in the questions and answers of
       students?

24.   appear interested in each student?

25.   approach students to help without being asked?

The first report card in Chapter 5 will help you
summarize your assessment of the effectiveness of the
teaching.

Chapter Four

As school is beginning, help your child succeed

Chapter 4

Part 9:
You're a Critical Member
of a Team Effort

Helping your child succeed requires a team effort. The team includes the student, the teachers, the administrators, and, very importantly, you, the parent. A successful team effort requires working together:

> setting goals together,
>
> deciding what has to be done and who is responsible for each action,
>
> following up on the status of planned actions,
>
> discussing each person's perceptions,
>
> promptly identifying or heading off problems,
>
> and modifying plans to keep on track.

Take the lead.

Set up meetings with your child's teacher whenever you feel the need. Establish and communicate the objectives for the meetings to the teacher. Communicate your understanding of your child's individual characteristics. Working together, you can agree on your child's strengths and areas that need improvement, and agree on a strategy that will bring out the best in your child. Following are some tips to help you build an effective working relationship with the school.

Plan your strategy.

1.   Plan the goals for skill development.

Determine with the teacher the skills and knowledge your child should be working on during the school year and what roles each of you (teacher, parent, student) will play to ensure that these skills and knowledge are acquired. Answering the following three questions will help:

a.   What skills and knowledge does the teacher intend the students to acquire by the end of the year?

b.   What skills and knowledge does your child bring to the class?

c.   Which skills does your child need to acquire by the end of the year?

2.   **Plan the strategy for skill development.**

Determine in specific terms what each person
(teacher, parent, student) can do to help the
student succeed.

With which skills does your child enter the class?
Determine what actions can be taken and what
adjustments can be made to keep the student
interested and growing.

3.   **Plan the strategy for working effectively with
your child.**

What type of interactions with adults bring out the
best in your child? Think about what your child is
like and what you have learned that does and does
not work, and communicate that to the teacher.
Develop a strategy that incorporates this
sensitivity to your child.

4.   **Plan the strategy for monitoring how well
things are going.**

Set up a strategy for monitoring how things are
going and for keeping in touch with each other.
Identify warning signals and talk about strategies
to head off problems.   Make appointments ahead
of time for meetings on a periodic basis.

Monitor, evaluate, and head off problems.

You've done some important preparatory work. Now the challenge--making it work . . .

Stay in touch with how things are going. Try to prevent problems from occurring. Using the principles and criteria described in this book, monitor and evaluate your child's work, your child's feelings, your child's behavior, and the teacher's perceptions.

Schedule meetings on a routine basis, asking the teachers to bring to the meeting:

> a description of what your child is doing well and specific suggestions for improvements,
>
> a description of actions the teachers have taken to help your child succeed,
>
> suggestions for what everyone (the teachers, the student, *and* the parents) might do differently to help your child succeed.
>
> Monitor your child's progress and the actions being taken. There are a number of techniques you can use. For example, rather than waiting for the results on tests, have your child take to each teacher an evaluation form on a weekly basis, and then bring the completed form to you. This ensures ongoing communication between the student, the teacher, and you. Also, make

appointments through the principal to observe the class for an afternoon or morning to get a sense of what is happening. Sit quietly in the back, borrow a text, if that would help, and evaluate the situation.

Listen to yourself. Listen to your intuition. Try to communicate clearly with the teachers--including both what seems to be going well and suggestions for improvements.

Part 10:
Do You Have Concerns About Your
Child's Current Situation?

Focus on the issues and the future.

When problems exist in most situations, usually more than
one person has helped contribute to the problem.
Certainly, focusing on what needs to be done in the
future, rather than blaming for past actions, will best use
everyone's time in solving the problems, and best
contribute to helping the student succeed.

If a student is not doing well on tests, for example, that is
a symptom of a problem. It may or may not mean that the
student is doing something wrong. Poor grades are
symptoms that something is wrong. The factors that are
causing poor grades still need to be determined. Solving
the problems is everyone's responsibility: the student, the
teacher, and the parent.

You are critical to helping solve the problems and helping
the student succeed. The way you handle the discussions
with the teachers is important. The discussions can be
constructive and productive. Actions can be taken and
changes can be made by all team members to help the
student acquire the skills and knowledge.

You should end up feeling comfortable with your
understanding of what is said and with the resolution to

the problem. Keep the goal of helping your child succeed
in mind. Concentrate on what activities must take place in
the future; conclude with a strategy that includes, for
each individual (e.g., parent, teacher, student, principal),
specific actions that will be taken, dates by which the
actions will be taken, and a follow-up meeting to check on
the status.

Identify the problems and possible solutions.

1. **Listen first--talk later.**

   Initially, your role is to gather information.
   Gather information from the student, from the
   teacher, and, as needed, from the principal. Ask
   questions and listen to the answers. Listening and
   jotting down answers will give you lots of needed
   information to help you solve the problem.

   You may be tempted to express your emotions
   about the teacher to the teacher, or to
   immediately respond to answers with which you
   disagree. Wait to respond until you have analyzed
   the problems.

   Draw out both your child and the teacher on
   issues such as the following:

   > What do they perceive the problem to be?

   > What factors are contributing to the
   > problem?

What actions have they taken to address the problem?

What could each of us do differently to address the problem?

You will identify more questions. These are just a starting point.

2. **Analyze the problems.**

Concentrate on developing an understanding of the problem:

a. The symptoms (indicators that something isn't going well)

Examples include poor grades, the student not wanting to go to class or to school, etc.

b. The problems (what's not being done or not being done effectively by each of you: the parent, the student, the teacher, and even the principal)

Examples include the student not making it clear to the teacher that he/she doesn't understand something; the teacher not making clear what is to be learned and the criteria for evaluation; the parent not listening when the student tries to communicate.

c.   The consequences (results of the
        problems)

        Examples include grades getting worse,
        student learning less, student getting
        bored, student misbehaving in class, etc.

d.   The causes of the problems (factors which
        lead to the problems)

        Examples include:

        not realizing that carrying out an action is
        one's responsibility (e.g., the student
        doesn't realize that he or she should
        indicate to the teacher or parent when he/
        she is getting confused and behind),

        not having skill and knowledge to keep up
        with the teacher's pace, or finding it
        unpleasant for some reason to do what
        someone else expects.

e.   The solutions (actions that each person
        can take to solve the problem)

        Examples include :

        the student clarifying what he/she does not
        understand, making a list, and discussing
        the issues with the teacher;

        the teacher making clear what is to be
        learned and the criteria for evaluation;

the parent responding to the student in a way that makes the student feel that he or she is being heard.

3. Communicate and discuss your analysis.

Present your thoughts as a springboard from which you and the teacher can talk. Try to identify perceptions of issues that you have in common and build on those commonalities.

If you feel that your child is being blamed, respond by saying something like "the student may not be doing everything right, but let's reserve judgment until we have a handle on the entire issue."

If you have questions or concerns about what the teacher is doing, try to avoid conveying emotion such as anger or blame to the teacher. Although doing so will probably make you feel better temporarily, it is also likely to make the teacher angry or defensive, which won't help you solve the problems. Try to indicate support for the teacher's intentions and an understanding of the constraints under which the teacher works.

Draw out the teacher's perceptions of your ideas.

Give visual indications that you are listening to the other person's ideas. Actions such as making eye contact and writing down what people are saying make others aware that they are being heard.

Keep the discussion on target; in other words, talk about the analysis of the problems and strategies to address them. Keep the goal in mind (to help your child succeed).

You don't have to solve the problems in one meeting. If the meeting is not going well or you feel that you need time to think about the issues or to discuss them with your spouse or a friend, stop the meeting at this juncture and set up an appointment for another meeting.

Spell out the goals and specific future actions.

Concentrate on developing goals and strategies for helping solve existing problems and for helping prevent future ones.

Following is a list of questions which may help solve the problems:

1.   Is there more that could be done in the design of the course to help the student succeed?

   a.   Were the instructional objectives distributed at the beginning of the course?

   b.   Are the expected performance and the criteria defined explicitly so that the student understands them?

    c.   What are the instructional objectives to which the tests relate?

    d.   Do the tests match the instructional objectives?

2.   Is there more the teacher could do to help the student acquire the needed skills and knowledge?

    a.   Were guidelines provided?

    b.   Were examples provided?

    c.   Were practice exercises provided?

    d.   Was feedback provided? Was the feedback immediate? Did it include aspects well done and specific suggestions for improvements?

    e.   Were questions of clarification encouraged?

    f.   Did the student have sufficient time to acquire the skills and knowledge given his/her entry knowledge?

    g.   Is the student representative of the group for whom the course was designed (in terms of skills and knowledge)? If not, did the teacher meet with the parent and student to make explicit the skills and knowledge the student needs to acquire?

Did the teacher determine with the parent and make needed adjustments in class assignments and assistance provided?

3.   Is there more the student could do to acquire the skills and knowledge?

a.   Did the student take tangible steps to define what he/she did and did not understand--from the beginning?

b.   Did the student make clear to the teacher or the parent what he/she did not understand or where he/she was having difficulties at each juncture?

c.   Did the student make it clear to the teacher or the parent that he/she felt lost--before doing poorly on the test?

d.   Did the student discuss course concepts with the teacher and with other students after class hours?

e.   Did the student do the work on a regular basis?

f.   Did the student participate in group discussions?

g.   Did the student think about how to apply the information and concepts learned in specific, real-life situations?

4. **Is there more the parents could do to help the student acquire the skills and knowledge?**

a. Are there changes you could make in the home setting to ensure that the student has sufficient time to study after school?

b. Are there changes you could make in how you are responding to the student's efforts? Are you monitoring the student's progress closely enough? Are you giving the student effective encouragement and support at home?

Keep bringing the discussion of ideas into better focus, to ensure everyone either has the same goals or clearly understands each other's. The teacher's goals and your goals may appear the same on the surface, but be different at a deeper level.

For example, perhaps your child tests very high and the teacher wants the student to make all A's to "live up to his or her potential." You, on the other hand, may not consider all A's critical and want the child to live a life not totally concentrated on academics.

Or you may value athletics more than one of the teachers.

Or you may consider a well-adjusted child to be one enjoying him- or herself while a particular teacher may perceive a well-adjusted child to be one who is quiet in class.

What if you feel that you and the school aren't working effectively together to solve the problems?

It's critical to try to work with the teacher first. If, after communicating with the teacher, you feel that the issues aren't being approached rationally and constructively, then escalate the problem to the next highest level in the school. Organizations always have procedures for escalating problems to higher levels where they can be solved. Try to talk with the principal as constructively and rationally as possible.

There are all kinds of people with many different values. We are not all compatible with each other. In addition, in certain situations, even if the values are the same, the conditions in which people are working may not enable them to do what you feel is necessary to meet your child's needs and to help your child succeed.

You can try escalating the problem to even higher levels than the principal in a school system, if they exist. Otherwise, look around for a school in which the staff have goals and values more similar to yours, or in which the staff have the skills, time, and energy to help your child succeed.

You probably have more options than you realize in both the public and private sector. Explore what is available in your community. There may be alternative programs in your school system that you may not have explored, such as magnet-school programs. It may be that by paying a nominal tuition, you can enroll your child in a school in another district. If cost is a factor, you may find that tuition is more affordable for some private schools than others.

You may decide to try to make the situation work with this teacher in this school. You should be able to develop strategies which will, at a minimum, be constructive, not destructive, for your child. The strategies should include actions that you, the student, the teacher, and the principal will take to help the student succeed, and specific dates you will meet to assess how things are going and to make needed changes in your strategies.

What if you feel that you and the school have tried everything you can think of to help your child succeed and there are still problems? Explore the resources in your community. There are a variety of professionals with whom you can consult, ranging from learning disability specialists to psychologists.

Again, at all times, even if you are not sure of yourself because tangible evidence of problems may not be there, the best thing you can do is to listen to your intuition. You know your child best. You have the greatest concern for your child's success. You are the person ultimately responsible for helping your child succeed.

Chapter
Five

Report Cards
to Evaluate Schools

Chapter 5
Report Cards
to Evaluate Schools

Chapter 5 includes three report cards to use to
evaluate schools:

Report Card 1:
   Assess the effectiveness of the teaching

Report Card 2:
   Summarize information about each school

Report Card 3:
Compare schools to each other

Report Card 1: Assess the Effectiveness of the Teaching

Factors to Consider	Very Effective			Needs Great Improvement		Comments: Aspects Well Done *and* Suggestions for Improvements
	1	2	3	4	5	
School Setting						
1. Teachers have the time and administrative support for good teaching.						
2. Teachers and principals demonstrate in their actions that they have the goal of helping the child succeed.						
3. Team members are communicating with each other.						
4. Team members are raising concerns forthrightly and are addressing them promptly and constructively.						
5. Team members are making changes as needed to help achieve the goal, i.e., to help the student succeed.						
6. Team members monitor the situation to help keep on target.						

Factors to Consider	Very Effective			Needs Great Improvement		Comments: Aspects Well Done *and* Suggestions for Improvements
	1	2	3	4	5	
Principal's and teachers' relationships with parents						
7. You feel comfortable asking them questions for information and questions for clarification.						
8. Educational jargon is paraphrased so you understand.						
9. Exchanges in communication result in both of you understanding the other more clearly and with a mutually agreed upon conclusion.						
10. Parents and teachers (and, as appropriate, students) set goals together.						
11. Teachers and principals encourage the development of specific plans for what should be done to help student succeed and who is responsible for each action.						
12. Teachers and principals encourage and ensure follow up to help student succeed.						

Factors to Consider	Very Effective			Needs Great Improvement		Comments: Aspects Well Done *and* Suggestions for Improvements
	1	2	3	4	5	
13. Teachers and principals communicate their perceptions and listen to parents.						
14. Teachers and principals both are receptive to and initiate actions which promptly identify and head off problems.						
15. Teachers and principals support modifying plans to keep on track--help the students succeed.						
Effectiveness of the design of the teaching						
16. Are there instructional objectives?						
17. Do the objectives include both the performance expected and the criteria?						
18. What are the entry skills (intellectual and interpersonal) of the majority of students?						
19. How do the skills of my child compare to those?						

Factors to Consider	Very Effective			Needs Great Improvement		Comments: Aspects Well Done *and* Suggestions for Improvements
	1	2	3	4	5	
20. Are the objectives appropriate for the majority of the students–sufficiently challenging, without overwhelming them?						
21. Are the objectives appropriate for my child?						
22. Do the objectives have the students thinking and applying, or reciting back facts?						
Effectiveness of the day-to-day instructional experiences						
23. Are needed information and guidelines provided?						
24. Are examples provided?						
25. Are practice exercises provided?						
26. Do the information provided, the guidelines, the demonstrations, and also the practice exercises pertain to the objectives?						

Factors to Consider	Very Effective			Needs Great Improvement		Comments: Aspects Well Done *and* Suggestions for Improvements
	1	2	3	4	5	
27. Are there sufficient opportunities to practice so the students can acquire the skills?						
28. How proficient do the students become at the skills?						
29. Are students given a sufficient number of opportunities to practice and sufficient feedback so they can improve?						
30. Are students given feedback that is specific and constructive? Does feedback include descriptions of aspects well done and specific suggestions for improvements?						
31. Are students encouraged to ask questions about what they still do not understand?						
32. Do answers appear to be clear and non-judgmental?						

Factors to Consider	Very Effective		Needs Great Improvement			Comments: Aspects Well Done *and* Suggestions for Improvements
	1	2	3	4	5	
Development of student's sense of responsibility						
33. Are students told to take tangible steps to define what they don't understand?						
34. Are students encouraged to make clear to the teacher what they don't understand at that moment in time?						
35. Are the students held accountable for work on a day-to-day basis?						
Assessment of student progress						
36. Do the teachers hold students responsible for performing?						
37. Is the assessment of student progress based on the instructional objectives? Do the tests match the instructional objectives?						

Factors to Consider	Very Effective			Needs Great Improvement		Comments: Aspects Well Done *and* Suggestions for Improvements
	1	2	3	4	5	
38. Are grades based on how well students performed according to the objectives?						
Extent to which individual student needs are met						
39. Do the teachers give feedback on individual work often? Does the feedback seem appropriate and constructive for each student?						
40. Do the teachers adjust the teaching techniques, based on what is working or not working with each student?						
Extent to which thinking is encouraged						
41. Are the teachers encouraging thinking? Do they supplement information, guidelines, and demonstration with opportunities to practice?						
42. Do the teachers provide students with sufficient practice needed to acquire skills?						

Factors to Consider	Very Effective			Needs Great Improvement		Comments: Aspects Well Done *and* Suggestions for Improvements
	1	2	3	4	5	
43. Do the teachers help students learn where to look for information and answers to their questions, rather than emphasizing memorization of facts independent of thinking?						
Manner of the teacher						
44. Does the teacher:						
a. Greet students warmly?						
b. Act friendly and non-threatening?						
c. Provide encouraging responses when students ask questions?						
d. Respond in a non-judgemental manner with ideas appropriate for the level of the student?						
e. Appear interested in the answers of each student?						
f. Appear interested in each student?						

Factors to Consider	Very Effective			Needs Great Improvement		Comments: Aspects Well Done *and* Suggestions for Improvements
	1	2	3	4	5	
g. Approach students to help without being asked?						
h. Individualize treatment of individuals to bring out the best in them?						
i. Maintain order in an authoritative and constructive manner?						

Report Card 2:
Summarize Information About Each School

Name

Address

Phone

Director's Name

Grades

Student & Post-Graduate Accomplishments

Teacher Performance

Parental Involvement

Discipline

School Resources

Educational Opportunities : Availability and frequency of programs such as language, music, fine arts, physical education, computers, history, arts, science, and bi-lingual

Transportation Arrangements

Application/Admissions Procedures

Summary of Costs:

Expenses: Comments:

Application fee: _____

Annual tuition: _____

Registration fee: _____

Books and supplies: _____

If uniforms required: _____

Transportation   _____

After-school care: _____

Summer school: _____

Administration fees: _____

**e.g., for paying tuition
over time**

**Other fees, e.g, art, field
trips, recreation**   _____

Total   _____

Report Card 3:
Compare Schools to Each Other

Major Factors	Schools
Student/post-graduate accomplishments	
Teacher performance	
Effectiveness of teaching	
Parental involvement	
Discipline	
School Resources	
Educational Opportunities	
Admission	
Costs	

USEFUL
REFERENCES AND
RESOURCES

USEFUL REFERENCES AND RESOURCES

Alvino, James, **Parents' Guide to Raising A Gifted Child**, Little, Brown, & Company; Boston and Toronto, 1985

> Dr. James Alvino, publisher and editor-in-chief of *Gifted Children Monthly* describes many techniques for helping gifted children succeed. Many of the suggestions Dr. Alvino makes may be helpful in raising any child.

Crossroads in American Education, Report No. 17-OV-01, National Assessment of Educational Progress, Educational Testing Service, Rosedale Road, Princeton, New Jersey 08541-0001, 1989

> This report provides an overview of findings from recent national assessments of schools in the United States in a variety of subject matter areas. The analysis of the subject matter areas may be useful to parents in helping assess some of the skills their children could be acquiring.

Feldman, Beverly Neuer, **Kids Who Succeed**, Rawson Associates, New York and Collier Macmillan, Canada, Inc., 1987

> Dr. Beverly Neuer Feldman describes methods for encouraging and developing skills in children for being independent and succeeding at endeavors.

Fisher, Roger and Ury, William, **Getting to Yes**, Penguin Group, Viking Penguin Inc., 40 West 23rd Street, N. Y., N.Y. 10010, 1983

>   Roger Fisher and William Ury describe a useful step-by-step procedure for discussing issues that are controversial and for arriving at mutually acceptable conclusions.

Harrison, Charles, **Public Schools U S A , A Comparative Guide to Schoool Districts**, Williamson Publishing, Charlotte, Vermont, 1988

>   Charles Harrison has organized an information base to enable parents to compare school districts surrounding major metropolitan areas in the United States.

Holt, John, **How Children Learn**, Dell Publishing, The Bantam Doubleday Publishing Group, Inc., N.Y., N.Y., 1967, 1983

>   John Holt describes the learning process and how to nurture emotional and intellectual growth.

Maeroff, Gene I., **The School-Smart Parent**, Times Books, Random House, Inc., N.Y., N.Y., 1989

>   Gene Maeroff provides information on what your child should be learning in pre-school, and kindergarten through sixth grade, and the essentials of science, math, social studies, and language.

Nault, William H., **Typical Course of Study**, World Book, Inc., 510 Merchandise Mart, Chicago, Illinois 60654, 1982

> Dr. Nault has developed an easily-referenced booklet that lists a synthesis of the major subject areas and topics covered for grades K-12. This booklet may be a useful resource for both evaluating or identifying the activities in a school parents may want to supplement.

National Committee for Citizens in Education, **Network for Public Schools**, 10840 Little Patuxent Parkway, Suite 301, Columbia, Maryland 20144

> The National Committee for Citizens in Education (NCCE), a non-profit organization, publishes this newsletter. The newsletter highlights issues relevant to parents and teachers, creative teaching endeavors, and useful references and books. Membership information can be obtained by writing them or calling 301-997-9300.

NCCE also maintains an information clearinghouse on school-based management, and improvement. For more information, call NCCE's hotline, 1-800-NETWORK.

Rich, Dorothy, **Megaskills**, Houghton Mifflin Company, 2 Park Street, Boston, Massachusetts 02108, 1988

> Dr. Rich describes many activities that parents and teachers can use to develop children's abilities to learn and to succeed not only in school, but beyond.

Schimmel, David and Fischer, Louis, **Parents, Schools and the Law**, 1987

> This book answers more than 200 questions about parents' rights and the law in school situations, including discipline, free speech, religion, education of the handicapped and gifted, and racial and sexual equality.

Sobol, Tom and Sobol, Harriet, **Your Child In School -- Kindergarten Through Second Grade**, Arbor House, William Morrow and Company, 105 Madison Avenue, N.Y., N.Y. 10016, 1988

Sobol, Tom and Sobol, Harriet, **Your Child In School -- Third Through Fifth Grade**, Arbor House, William Morrow and Company, 105 Madison Avenue, N.Y., N.Y. 10016, 1988

> Harriet and Tom Sobol describe how young children learn and what can be done to facilitate their learning.

What Students Need to Know, National Urban League, 1988

> This guide describes academic subjects and basic competencies (writing, listening, reasoning, computer usage) students need to succeed in school now and later on the job.

To improve the quality of our publications we would appreciate your input. . . .

This book was developed as a result of discussions with many parents. We would appreciate your taking a few minutes to answer the questions below. When you send us suggestions for improvements, we will add your name to our mailing list to keep you informed about upcoming products.

Please feel free to make any suggestions for improvements in future editions of *Help Your Child Succeed in School* and send them to:

The Clarendon Group, Inc.

Suite 340

2480-4 Briarcliff Road

Atlanta, Georgia 30329

1. Before reading this book, how much formal training in Education did you have?

    a. Master's degree or above

    b. Bachelor's degree

    c. Some training

    d. None at all

2. What is your educational background?

    a. High-school degree or equivalent

    b. Bachelor's degree

    c. Master's degree

    d. Doctorate or equivalent

3. What are your children's ages?_____

4. Why did you purchase this book?

5. Did this book meet your needs?_____

a. If so, what aspects of the book were useful?

b. If not, what aspects of the book could be improved? (Please give specific suggestions to improve clarity, to help ensure that suggestions are useful, and to help ensure that the book is easy to use.)

c. What lessons have you learned,as a parent helping your child succeed in school that you would be willing to share with other parents? In other words, what did we leave out?

d. What references and other resources do you think would be helpful to parents?

7. Any additional ideas or suggestions :

Please print:

Name_____

Address_____

City_____State_____Zip_____

Telephone__(____)_____

FOR MORE INFORMATION

Books and products

from The Clarendon Group, Inc.

Help Your Child Succeed in School A book designed for parents to help influence how their child is taught. Will be useful to parents whether they are looking for schools, dissatisfied with the current situation, or just trying to make a good situation better. Includes indispensable and time-saving checklists, tools, and recommendations for getting the most out of parent/teacher conferences. Concise, clear, and easy-to use, this book offers critical information not available elsewhere.

Parent's Action Resource Kit   A collection of Report Cards, sample meeting agendas for parent/teacher conferences, and sample letters for communicating effectively with the schools.   Also included is a sample evaluation form parents can use to have their child take to the teachers on a weekly or monthly basis to ensure clear communication about the child's performance.   All of the materials in the packet are in work-book (8 1/2 x 11) format, including 15 copies each of the three (3) Report Cards included in the book, **Help Your Child Succeed in School.** This collection is designed to enable the parent to be well prepared for interactions with a school.

Parent's Pocket Action Plan A "pocket" reference to assist parents in planning for and participating in parent/ teacher conferences. Includes needed information for three (3) major steps: *Plan Ahead* (and How to Ask the

Teacher to Prepare); *Questions to Ask During the Conference*; and *Conclude the Conference with An Action Plan.*

Super-Teaching: How to Help Your Students Learn A book for individuals who have been asked to teach, but have no formal training in Education. The book includes step-by-step guidelines for systematically planning and designing effective instructional programs and for enabling the teacher to carry out self-evaluations.

A Teacher's Report Cards A collection of 100 copies each in 8 1/2 x 11 format of the Teacher's Report Card included in the book, **Super-Teaching: How to Help Your Students Learn.** This Report Card, ready for distribution to students, will enable teachers to receive constructive and helpful feedback and evaluate their own teaching.

ORDER FORM

The Clarendon Group, Inc.

Suite 340

2480-4 Briarcliff Road

Atlanta, Georgia 30329

Telephone (404)-284-7012

Fax: (404)-284-7028

Please send me the following books and products:

____ Help Your Child Succeed in School		$16.95
____ Parent's Action Resource Kit		$14.95
____ Parent's Pocket Action Plan		$ 4.95
____ Super-Teaching:		
How to Help Your Students Learn		$19.95
____A Teacher's Report Cards		$10.95

I understand that I may return any product within 10 days for a full refund if not satisfied.

Please print:

Name:_____

Address:_____

_____Zip:_____

Please enclose payment (check or money order; no cash please).

Georgians: Please add 5% sales tax.

Shipping and handling: $2.00 for **each** product.

_____I don't want to wait 3-4 weeks for Book Rate mailing. Here is $3.00 for **each** book for Air Mail postage.

ORDER FORM

The Clarendon Group, Inc.
Suite 340
2480-4 Briarcliff Road
Atlanta, Georgia 30329
Telephone (404)-284-7012
Fax (404)-284-7028

Please send me the following books and products:

____ Help Your Child Succeed in School	$16.95
____ Parent's Action Resource Kit	$14.95
____ Parent's Pocket Action Plan	$ 4.95
____ Super-Teaching:	
How to Help Your Students Learn	$19.95
____A Teacher's Report Cards	$10.95

I understand that I may return any product within 10 days for a full refund if not satisfied.

Please print:

Name:_____

Address:_____

_____Zip:_____

Please enclose payment (check or money order; no cash please).
Georgians: Please add 5% sales tax.
Shipping and handling: $2.00 for **each** product.

_____ I don't want to wait 3-4 weeks for Book Rate mailing. Here is $3.00 for **each** book for Air Mail postage.